A Ferret Named Phil

Copyright © 2015 William Reimer. All Rights Reserved.

Third edition.

First published in hardcover in 2015 in Australia
by Liberty Road Studios ABN 13 576 424 374

Re-issued in softcover in 2017

This book is copyright. Apart from any fair dealing for the purposes of private use, criticism or review, as permitted under the Copyright Act, no part may be reproduced by any process without written permission. Inquiries should be addressed to the publisher.

ISBN 978-0-9942950-0-2

To learn more, find us on Facebook or visit
www.aferretnamedphil.com.au

A Ferret Named Phil

William Reimer

illustrations by
James Moore

To every child, parent and teacher,

*May this lighthearted book spark the much-needed conversation about bullying.
May it encourage discussion of the many different ways to address it,
and may it empower those who face it.*

~ William Reimer

There once was a ferret, a ferret named Phil.
His mother was Shirley, his father was Bill.
They all lived together, inside an old mill,
and as far as I know, they are living there still.

On a bright sunny day, Phil climbed out of bed. He raced to the kitchen, his cap on his head. *"Morning dear Phil"* said his mother Shirley "Morning" said Bill. *"You're up rather early!"*

"Yes Dad," said Phil. "I'm off to see Jane."
"We're going out to the lake, it had better not rain!"
"But Phil, isn't that where the mean Hugo plays?"
"Yes Mum," said Phil. "But I'm not afraid."

"Now please tell us Phil, what will you say,
if Hugo the hawk picks on you today?"
"I'll tell him—No, go away, leave me alone."
"That's right," said Bill. "And if he does, let us know."

Phil strolled off to see Jane on his usual route,
after eating his breakfast, with plenty of fruit.
He met up with Jane and they walked to the lake.
They sang ferret songs and ate carrot cake.

All of a sudden, from the far distant creek
Phil heard the sound of a very loud shriek.
He turned towards Jane, but before he could talk,
down flew Hugo, the big scary hawk.

Hugo was mean, as mean as could be,
he was often found perched on top of his tree.
He picked on the weak, he picked on the small,
he picked on the poor ferret Phil, most of all.

"Hello there Phil," Hugo slowly did say,
"what food do you have for me today?"
Phil replied swiftly "I've nothing for you,
so please go away, and stay away too!"

The hawk stood up sharply, and flapped his great wings, sending into the lake all of Phil and Jane's things!
"Phil you've been silly... now look what you've done!"
Hugo was smiling, but Jane was quite glum.

*"To teach you a lesson, I'll take Jane away…
and maybe next time you might do as I say!"*
Hugo took Jane, to Phil's disbelief,
up to his treehouse, and onto a leaf.

"Please help me Phil!" Jane cried from the skies.
"Jane!" shouted Phil, with tears in his eyes.
As fast as he could, Phil climbed up the tree,
but fell down and grazed his poor ferret knee.

Hugo the hawk was feeling quite pleased.
"You small silly ferret" the cruel Hugo teased.
"Jane, hold on tight, I'll think of a way!"
Jane replied, *"Phil, I don't have all day..."*

Phil collected his friends, and with his smart mind,
they gathered up all of the sticks they could find!
They worked through the day, it was a wonderful sight.
They built a great ladder, of a very great height.

Suddenly Phil heard an owl calling *"Hoot!"*
And he had an idea while he munched on some fruit.
Being a ferret, Phil was quite wise.
He decided to build a big owl disguise.

He told all his friends, and with plenty of feathers,
in just a few hours they had built it together.
It was ready by midnight, they were all rather proud.
They crept up the ladder, trying not to be loud.

Huddled together, inside their owl suit,
Phil whispered 4, 3, 2, 1, then they gave a great *"Hoot!"*
Hugo the hawk gave a great squeal of fright,
then he leapt from his perch and flew into the night!

Feeling relieved, Phil smiled at Jane.
Jane said to Phil, *"Nice to see you again."*
Slowly but surely, they climbed down the tree.
Phil said to Jane, *"Would you care for some tea?"*

So off they both walked, all the way to the mill,
and that was the tale of a ferret named Phil.

PS

The lesson Phil learnt was worth more than gold.

To stand up for himself, to be brave, and be bold.

Phil is still friends with Jane, they meet now and then.

As for Hugo the hawk? He never picked on Phil again.

CPSIA information can be obtained at www.ICGtesting.com
Printed in the USA
LVIW01n1523091018
592925LV00008B/22